D1208497

GOLF COURSE DESIGNS BY FAZIO

Introduction

For several years, friends and associates have suggested that we put together a sampling of the golf courses we have designed, a collection that illustrates different design concepts and styles. Although we have designed close to 100 golf courses over the past 20 years, the task of selecting just a few of these to include in a book seemed almost impossible, and there has never seemed to be sufficient time nor a suitable format to do so.

This book is an attempt to answer these requests. The selections are dictated as much as anything by the available photographs. There will be future editions that will include other Fazio courses. This book is largely photographic because it seemed the best way to show the actual results of golf course design. Schematic and architectural plans are not easily read by golf enthusiasts, while photographs capture the many moods and visual images of golf in a way we like to remember.

The design of a golf course is a collaboration of the client, the architect and mother nature. This leads to an almost infinite variety of design influences, objectives and aesthetic considerations. The art of golf course design lies in balancing these influences and blending them into a final product that is distinctive, appealing and playable. Sometimes the result is spectacular, like the cliff holes at the U.S. Virgin Islands, where nature provided a glorious setting and the client allowed us to use it. We have tried to portray variety by including many different types of courses with settings ranging from the ocean to the desert, from the mountains to the marshlands, from the islands to the parklands.

The brief text that accompanies each group of photographs describes the principal design influences and tells just enough about each golf course to orient the reader to its basic characteristics and theme.

We have been fortunate that, in all of the projects described in this book, we have been involved not only in the technical design but also in the actual construction and execution of the artistic concept. We believe that the long-term, personal involvement of the golf course designer is an important bridge as each new golf course emerges from the drawing board and is nurtured to life.

Cliff hole at U.S. Virgin Islands, 145 yards, par-3

The Vintage Club

Desert and mountains provide the principle influences for the design of the golf courses at The Vintage Club at Indian Wells, situated in the California desert near Palm Springs. The Mountain Course, the first of two for this exclusive community of private homes, opened for play in 1980. The holes are shaped from the flat desert sand, using a blend of modern and traditional design treatments. Huge mounds and abrupt, grassy bunkers lend to the course a distinct flavor of the old-style British courses, a device that works as a counterpoint to the rough-hewn mountain backdrop. Desert plantings provide visual and strategic exclamation points. Elements like greenside mounds and pot bunkers revive subtle playing values that enrich golf and are rooted in its origins. This reflects a sense of tradition felt by the founders of the club, who established in 1981 The Vintage Invitational, a prestigious Masters-style tournament for great senior professionals. The treacherous 16th and 17th holes thrust deep into the mountain cove past cascading waterfalls. Serpentine lakes are accented by bursts of desert flowers, a setting that Jimmy Demaret and Sam Snead have said is one of the most beautiful and distracting in golf.

OPENED FOR PLAY: 1980

7th Hole, The Vintage Club (Mountain Course), 159 yards, par-3

16th Hole, The Vintage Club (Mountain Course), 406 yards, par-4

The Vintage Club

17th Hole, The Vintage Club (Mountain Course), 144 yards, par-3

Golf Club of Oklahoma

The Golf Club of Oklahoma is situated on 525 acres of rolling plainsland outside Tulsa in the sleepy village of Broken Arrow, where a small group of investors wanted a private club devoted exclusively to the game of golf. The property is richly endowed with sandy loam soil, a 35-acre natural lake, ample tree cover, and the sort of naturally contoured landscape that lends itself to green settings and fairway shapes of great variety and golfing interest. With that large area to work with, there was complete freedom to take advantage of all the natural features the land offered. Holes meander through rolling plainsland, woods and ravines, some framed by sweeping fields of native grasses, others by glades of oak and river birch, or the wide open vistas of the large lake. The golf course occupies 130 acres, and another 40 acres is devoted to a practice facility which is one of the most luxurious in golf. It is shaded, offers four levels of tees, has a large putting clock, sand and grass bunkers, a huge chipping green with mounds and moguls, and as a crowning touch there are three complete practice holes of varying lengths surrounding the range. This facility reflects the passion for golf which allows its members to fully enjoy an hour or so of practice in relaxed seclusion. It is hard to recall another golf course in recent times that has been conceived and built with utter disregard for housing and real estate development, where the founders went out looking for the property solely for its suitability to the game of golf.

OPENED FOR PLAY: 1983

3rd Hole, Golf Club of Oklahoma, 415 yards, par-4

8th Hole, 593 yards, par-5

Golf Club of Oklahoma

5th Hole, Golf Club of Oklahoma, 205 yards, par-3

17th Hole, Golf Club of Oklahoma, 162 yards, par-3

PGA National

Our concept for the PGA National Golf Club called for three courses of varying style and degree of difficulty to form the centerpiece of the new headquarters complex for the PGA of America in Palm Beach Gardens, Florida. Two of our courses, The Haig and The Squire, were named after golf immortals Walter Hagen and Gene Sarazen. The Champion Course is the most testing and is a major tournament site for the PGA Championship and Ryder Cup matches. This meant creating a golf course of the sternest character and quality. The greens are designed to be on the small side with pronounced contours and undulations, a factor which elevates the test of golf to the highest level, regardless of weather. The typically flat South Florida terrain proved to be no barrier to achieving this. Indeed, many of the famous links of Great Britain emerged from land as flat and unpromising. In a sense, the site of the Championship Course offered an almost unlimited opportunity to create a great variety of challenging golf situations that encompass the full range of shot values.

OPENED FOR PLAY: 1980

3rd Hole, PGA National (Champion), 539 yards, par-5

1st Hole, PGA National (Champion Course), 369 yards, par-4

Pinehurst No. 6

Pinehurst is regarded as one of the shrines of American Golf, owing largely to the work of the late golf architect Donald Ross. It was here that Ross lived and created five wonderful golf courses, one of which, Pinehurst No. 2, is an acknowledged masterpiece. In designing a sixth course for this North Carolina resort complex, we were given terrain quite different from the gently-rolling sand hills that Ross shaped—relatively hilly, with more severe contours and elevation changes. Although there are visual similarities, Pinehurst No. 6 was designed as a complement to the existing five courses, not a copy. Examples are the hillside settings at each of the four par-3 holes, and the use of water and multiple tees which create wide flexibility in length and angle of difficulty. Pinehurst No. 6 is strong enough from the long tees, to have been used in qualifying for the professional tour, yet is most adaptable and playable for the handicap golfer, ranging from 5400 yards for women to 6400 yards for men. A link with the resort's older courses is provided by the native vegetation of magnolia, scrub oak, holly and pine and the characteristic pine needle carpets which frame the holes and evoke the unmistakable feel of Pinehurst.

OPENED FOR PLAY: 1976

2nd Hole, Pinehurst No. 6, 525 yards, par-5

9th Hole, Pinehurst Country Club No. 6, 437 yards, par-4

6th Hole, 500 yards, par-5

Butler National

In appearance, Butler National Golf Club has the inland, parkland characteristics of many midwestern golf courses, with little suggestion of toughness it actually possesses. Butler National is an all-men's club located within a unique sports core, the centerpiece of the late Paul Butler's development of a quality-oriented business park in the Chicago suburb of Oak Brook, Illinois. From the outset, the course was conceived as a difficult and sturdy test of golf that would serve both the business-oriented membership and as the site of the Western Open, America's second oldest championship. Because of this, Butler National was designed to have 18 strong holes. This strength lies sleeping in the placement of contours and bunkers. Small greens, renowned for their deceptive rolls, angle to the fairways to force correct placement of tee shots into preferred landing areas for approach shots. A small river, Salt Creek, runs through the property and enhances the challenge of approach shots on six holes. A lake comes into play on three holes, including the par-3 fifth, where the lake must be carried 205 yards from the back tee to a large peninsula green. Enhanced by its position as the permanent home of the Western Open, Butler National already has gained a national reputation and wide acceptance as one of the world's outstanding tests of golf.

OPENED FOR PLAY: 1972

8th Hole, looking back from green to tee.

8th Hole, Butler National Golf Club, 178 yards, par-5

Butler National

7th Hole, Butler National Golf Club, 603 yards, par-5

5th Hole, Butler National Golf Club, 205 yards, par-3

Jupiter Hills

The setting for the Jupiter Hills Club is almost unique in Florida, owing to huge sand hills that crest up to 60 and 70 feet above the nearby ocean. Because of this natural-terrain blessing, the course is distinguished by startling elevations. Holes tumble from lofty tee perches or climb, sometimes forbiddingly, to sentinel-like greens, many of them defended by yawning sand craters. Jupiter Hills was founded in 1969 and is surrounded by a state nature preserve, whose natural beauty and look are mirrored in the layout of the holes. Ranked among the top two dozen in America, Jupiter Hills is a relentless test of golf which plays longer than its measured distance of 6850 yards. Narrow, tree-lined fairways, ocean breezes and fast twisting greens are constant factors in club selection. The finishing hole sweeps 420 yards from the crest of one colossal dune, through a deep, richly carpeted depression, to the summit of another, where the visual rewards are unmatched in South Florida.

OPENED FOR PLAY: 1970

2nd Hole, Jupiter Hills Club, 440 yards, par-4

Jupiter Hills

9th Hole, Jupiter Hills Club, 192 yards, par-3

18th Hole, Jupiter Hills Club, 420 yards, par-4

Palmetto Dunes

Natural features are not always the most critical in establishing the design concept for a golf course. An example is the Fazio Course at Palmetto Dunes, the beach resort and residential complex on Hilton Head Island, S. C. With a resort-style course already in place, the developers wanted a difficult second course as a counterpart and a potential tournament site. But there were only 119 acres available, and to put a strong test of golf on this restricted area led to a number of design decisions. First, the course was designed as a par-70 of 6,800 yards which, in terms of playability is more difficult than a par-72 course over the same distance. Also, the course would have to be relatively narrow. To compensate for the average golfer, who tends to slice, the routing was set up so that there would be no out-of-bounds on the right side. The Island's thick semi-tropical vegetation and sandy soil, together with man-made waterways and canals that lace the property, were used as natural backdrops and strategic hazards. The premium is on driving accuracy and pinpoint long iron shots. Soon after its completion, the Fazio Course at Palmetto Dunes gained national recognition when it was selected in Golf Digest's list of America's 100 greatest tests of golf.

OPENED FOR PLAY: 1973

17th Hole, Palmetto Dunes (Fazio Course), 222 yards, par-3

4th Hole, Palmetto Dunes (Fazio Course), 197 yards, par-3

Champions

When Jimmy Demaret and Jack Burke, Jr. developed their now-famous Champions Golf Club in Houston, they wanted two 18-hole courses of equal challenge, but of quite different character. The first 18, Cypress Creek, was laid out in a modern concept that features length and huge flat greens. In designing the second, The Jack Rabbit, our commission was to follow the style of the great eastern courses — narrower fairways and medium-sized, elevated greens. The terrain is Texas flat, with pine and oak forests, so lakes were created to provide visual beauty and strategic obstacles as well as material for building up the green sites. The challenge was to provide an emphasis on shot-making which was achieved through the angles and shapes of greens. Tight driving holes, dogleg fairways and deep greenside bunkers enhance the eastern flavor. The 18th hole, a 557-yard par-5, was selected in Sports Illustrated's compilation of America's best 18 holes.

OPENED FOR PLAY: 1964

18th Hole, 557 yards, par-5

11th Hole, Champions Golf Club (Jack Rabbit), 196 yards, par-3

Moselem Springs

In the rural hill country of eastern Pennsylvania, nature has fashioned a noble scenery of broad vistas. Rolling waves of woodland and meadows sweep across the valleys and hills toward distant mountains, a landscape of grandeur and solitude that is ideal for golf. In this setting, near the village of Reading, is the Moselem Springs Golf Club, conceived as a club with a small, private membership devoted to quality and golf. The property contains an unusual variety of land forms, including abandoned quarries and deep natural depressions, which provide interest and challenge and permit a great variety in types of golf holes. The site offered many opportunities to establish elevated tee positions, which command spectacular views of the distant landscape and heighten the feeling of expanse. The course is further defined by creeks, rolling hillsides and densely wooded areas, where some holes appear as welcome corridors of utter seclusion. Moselem Springs plays to a par of 70 and is ranked in the top 100 of America's courses. The long driveway that approaches the clubhouse winds through several magnificently maintained holes. With no homes around the property to intrude on the setting, there is a distinct feeling of entering a true golf retreat.

OPENED FOR PLAY: 1965

10th Hole, Moselem Springs Golf Club, 403 yards, par-4

18th Hole, Moselem Springs Golf Club, 456 yards, par-4

Moselem Springs

13th Hole, Moselem Springs Golf Club, 208 yards, par-3

9th Hole, Moselem Springs Golf Club, 389 yards, par-4

Moss Creek

Moss Creek Plantation is a private residential retreat in the gracious southern style, located at Hilton Head Island, S.C., amid some of the most strikingly beautiful marshland settings on the Eastern Seaboard. The principal influences for the two golf courses at Moss Creek are luxuriant moss-draped forests and the open marshes and estuaries which flank the property. The two courses contrast in look and playability. The Devil's Elbow North is on the Scottish side, with a distinct look of older, more traditional golf courses. Greens, bunkers and hazards are designed on a moderate to small scale. The Devil's Elbow South is a more modern design, which moves through the forests and out along the silent marshes past the billowing natural grasses and serene beauty, which is the most impressive feature of the site. The Devil's Elbow South is the permanent site of the prestigious Women's International Tournament. The final holes, two of which are pictured here, play over and around the marshland and, more often than not, have proven decisive in the outcome of the tournament.

OPENED FOR PLAY: 1974

Detail, 15th hole

15th Hole, Moss Creek (Devil's Elbow South), 188 yards, par-3

Moss Creek

9th Hole, Moss Creek (Devil's Elbow North), 415 yards, par-4

7th Hole, Moss Creek (Devil's Elbow South), 174 yards, par-3

14th Hole, Moss Creek (Devil's Elbow North), 338 yards, par-4

Jonathan's Landing

Jonathan's Landing is a water-oriented golf community of private, clustered residences developed by Alcoa Properties adjacent to the Intercoastal Waterway in Jupiter, Florida. The peaceful effect of water on both golf and living areas is the unifying influence in the design of the golf course. Many lakes and canals were created and woven into the design of the holes. Length is not a major feature of the course. Instead, the layout stresses finesse and playability, in keeping with the concept that length alone is not necessary to create golfing interest and quality. While water is a strategic factor on some holes, it is also used to create visible reflective surfaces away from areas of play, to mirror the ever-changing palette of the skies and cloud formations which are such a constant and pleasing feature of South Florida.

OPENED FOR PLAY: 1978

9th Hole, 445 yards, par-4

General view, Jonathan's Landing Golf Club

Edgewood-Tahoe

The Edgewood-Tahoe golf course stretches along the edge of South Lake Tahoe amid some of the most magnificent scenery in golf. The holes are oriented so that the golfer will have frequent views of the snow-capped Sierra Nevada Mountains, which provide a distant and vivid backdrop. Located in a major resort area and serving many local hotels, the course was the site of the 1980 U.S. Publinx Championship. It is longer than most, stretching to some 7400 yards, to compensate for the thinner air of its 6200-foot elevation. The property straddles the California-Nevada state line, providing golfers with the novelty of starting the ninth hole in California and finishing in Nevada. The eighth hole, where the state line cuts through the middle of the green, offers putting from one state to the other. The course winds through forests where majestic Ponderosa pines rise 60 to 100 feet, and finishes along the edge of Lake Tahoe.

OPENED FOR PLAY: 1967

18th Hole, Edgewood-Tahoe Golf Course, 577 yards, par-5

Edgewood-Tahoe

12th Hole, Edgewood-Tahoe Golf Course, 213 yards, par

17th Hole, Edgewood-Tahoe Golf Course, 212 yards, par-3

The National

The National Club in Toronto, Canada, began as a men-only club and is designed to be a strong test of golf for the serious player. The terrain features large, rolling hills and valley settings. Holes twist in and out of these hills, hugging the sides, with several elevated tees providing expansive views. Its par 3 holes are all very strong and picturesque, leaving memorable images in the golfer's mind. The course is long, with large rolling greens and massive bunkers. It has been referred to as "Jaws" because of the wide-mouthed openings of its bunkers and the ferocity of the holes, a reputation which was upheld when the course was the site of the Canadian PGA Championship. The Club follows strict maintenance practices, including cutting the fairways with greens' mowers, upholding the members' prevailing attitude that, at The National, "golf is the only lauguage spoken."

OPENED FOR PLAY: 1974

18th Hole, The National Club, 414 yards, par-4

12th Hole, The National Club, 497 yards, par-5

4th Hole, 520 yards, par-5

Wild Dunes

The terrain and setting for Wild Dunes is the kind a golf course designer comes across only once or twice in a lifetime. Not only does it have massive oaks, pines, magnolias and cedar trees, but also serene marsh-front settings, massive interior sand dunes, and a finish that stretches along the broad expanse of beach beside the Atlantic Ocean. Wild Dunes Golf Links serves an active residential, vacation and resort community located on the Isle of Palms, one of a chain of barrier islands off the coast of South Carolina 15 miles from Charleston. Fascinating and dramatic contrasts in green settings were suggested by the terrain itself. Many of the holes look as if they had been there forever. One of these is the 11th, a narrow sliver of green fairway that undulates over dunesland past twisted old oaks; the only earth moved during construction of this hole was for the tee. Some of the interior holes evoke images of the mist-shrouded forests found in Ireland; others unfold in classic linksland form alongside the ocean. Measuring 6708 yards from the back tees, Wild Dunes, par-72, is ranked as one of the 50 greatest courses in the world by Golf Magazine's international panel of experts.

OPENED FOR PLAY: 1979

5th Hole, Wild Dunes Golf Links, 505 yards, par-5

12th Hole, Wild Dunes Golf Links, 192 yards, par-3

Wild Dunes

18th Hole, Wild Dunes Golf Links, 540 yards, par-5

Index & Credits

The Vintage Club (Mountain Course), page 4
Golf Club of Oklahoma, page 8
PGA National Golf Club (Champion Course), page 12
Pinehurst Country Club No. 6, page 14
Butler National Golf Club, page 16
Jupiter Hills Club, page 20
Palmetto Dunes (Fazio Course), page 24
Champions Golf Club (Jack Rabbit Course), page 26
Moselem Springs Golf Club, page 28
Moss Creek (Devil's Elbow), page 32
Jonathan's Landing, page 36
Edgewood-Tahoe Golf Course, page 38
The National Club, page 42
Wild Dunes Golf Links, page 44

Photo Credits

Virgin Islands
Paul Barton (page 3)

The Vintage Club
Tony Roberts (pages 4, 6-7)
Steve Szurlej (page 5)

G.C. of Oklahoma
Cal Brown (pages 8-9)
Tony Roberts (pages 10-11)

PGA National
Paul Barton (pages 12-13)

Pinehurst No. 6
Tony Roberts (pages 14, 15)

Butler National
Brian Morgan (pages 16, 18)
Tony Roberts (pages 17, 19)

Jupiter Hills
Cal Brown (pages 21, 23)
Tony Roberts (page 22)

Palmetto Dunes
Tony Roberts (pages 24, 25)

Champions
Cal Brown (pages 26-27)

Moselem Springs
Tony Roberts (pages 28-31)

Moss Creek
Drew Butler (pages 32-33)
Tony Roberts (pages 34 and 35, right)
Paul Barton (page 35, left)

Jonathan's Landing
Cal Brown (page 36)
Jeff Turnau (page 37)

Edgewood-Tahoe
Tony Roberts (pages 38-39, 40, 41)

The National
Brian Morgan (pages 42-43)

Wild Dunes
Tony Roberts (page 44)
William Cornelia (page 45)
Brian Morgan (pages 46-47)

Editorial and publishing direction:
Cal Brown

Book design and art direction:
Udo Machat

Sketches by Michael Strantz

Printed by Paragon Press, Salt Lake City